Deserts

Words by Carroll R. Norden, Ph.D.
Professor of Zoology
University of Wisconsin—Milwaukee

Raintree Childrens Books
Milwaukee • Toronto • Melbourne • London

Library of Congress Number: 77-27090

5 6 7 8 9 0 82 81

Printed and bound in the United States of America.

Library of Congress Cataloging in Publication Data

Norden, Carroll R.
   Deserts.

   (Read about)
   Bibliography: p.
   Includes index.
   SUMMARY: Describes the appearance, location,
inhabitants, and vegetation of deserts.
   1. Deserts—Juvenile literature. 2. Desert ecology—
Juvenile literature. [1. Deserts] I. Title.
GB611.M67   500.9'15'4   77-27090
ISBN 0-8393-0082-4 lib. bdg.

Deserts

More than one-third of the earth's land is desert. There are different kinds of deserts, but they all are very dry. Most deserts get less than 10 inches (25 centimeters) of rain a year.

Because there is so little rainfall, most plants do not grow well in the desert. And many plant-eating animals do not live in the desert because they cannot find enough food.

Often, strong winds blow across deserts. Sometimes the wind blows the sand into piles called dunes.

Some dunes stay in one place. Others are moved around by winds after they are formed. Dunes that stay in one place have plants growing on them. The roots of the plants help keep the dunes from being blown away.

There are different shapes and sizes of dunes. Some may be as small as 3 feet (1 meter) high. Other dunes may be over 1,300 feet (400 meters) high.

Some dunes are shaped like quarter moons. These are called barchans. In other places, the wind blows the sand into long parallel ridges. Dunes may also be shaped like an S or rounded at the top.

The most common kind of desert is made of rock. Different kinds and shapes of rock cover the desert floor. There may be hills or mountains made of rock. Sometimes the rock is full of tiny holes. Rainwater flows through the rock to the earth below.

The shape of desert rock can be changed by the wind, water, or by a rock slide. The rock is slowly worn away by sand being blown against it or by water running over it. It takes thousands of years to change the shape of the rock in this way.

Some deserts are
very cold. But like
other deserts, they
are dry and have
little plant or animal
life.

Cold deserts get
most of their water
in the form of snow.
The ground is
covered with snow
and ice most of
the year.

Some plants live through dry periods in the form of a seed buried under the ground. As soon as it rains, the seeds begin to grow. Shortly after the rain, the desert is covered with brightly colored flowers.

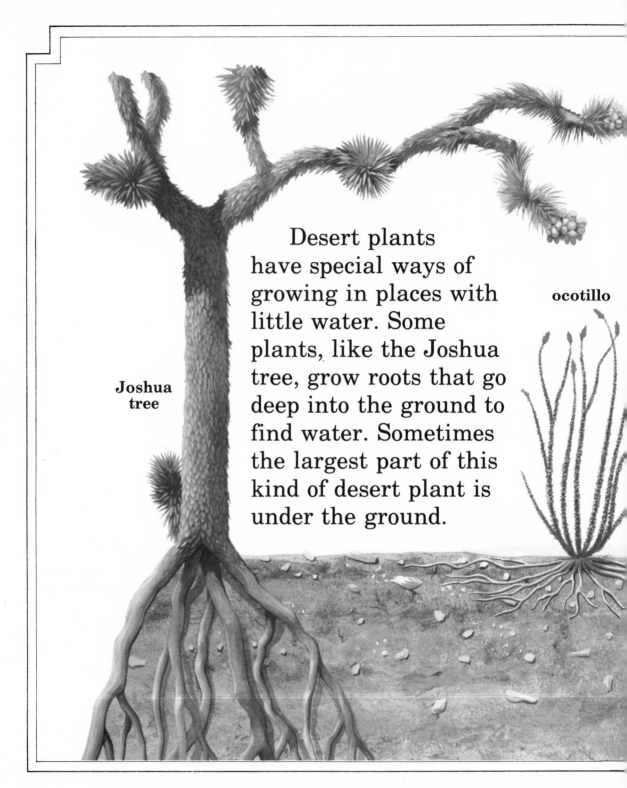

Desert plants
have special ways of
growing in places with
little water. Some
plants, like the Joshua
tree, grow roots that go
deep into the ground to
find water. Sometimes
the largest part of this
kind of desert plant is
under the ground.

Joshua
tree

ocotillo

Other plants, like the saguaro, grow huge roots just below the ground. Then when it rains, they are able to soak up water from a large area and store it in their stems. A layer of wax covering the stem helps keep the cactus from losing water.

saguaro

desert owl   kangaroo rat   rattlesnake

Many animals have learned special ways to live in a desert climate.

Some have scaly skin, which helps keep them from losing water.

Animals that live in hot deserts often spend the day in the shade, under rocks, or in a hole in the soil. At night they come out to hunt for food.

bobcat

Plant-eating
animals may move
from place to place
so that they can feed
on the plant growth
following rainfalls.

Some birds do not
have young in years
that are very dry,
because there would
not be enough food.

kit fox

elf owl

Because there are few tall trees in the desert, many birds must build nests on the ground. The elf owl often makes its nest in holes made by woodpeckers.

Jerboas rest during the day in holes. They dig the holes with their teeth and front claws. At night, they come out to look for food.

jerboa

Most frogs and toads are found near water holes in the desert. Some, like the spadefoot toad, dig a deep hole in the ground. They come out when it rains.

spadefoot toad

The desert scorpion is usually light brown or yellowish in color. The poisonous stinger at the end of its tail makes it one of the most dangerous desert animals.

scorpion

An oasis is a place in the desert that has a supply of fresh water. The water usually comes from under the ground.

Because of the water, an oasis is a gathering place for people and animals. Animals feed on the plants and grasses. And people grow crops in the shade in the oasis.

The date palm is
often grown in an
oasis. Its fruit is a
main source of food for
people and animals.
The wood of the palm
is used for building.
And its leaves can be
used for making roofs.

The Sahara desert is the largest desert in the world. Many different groups of people live in the Sahara.

One group of Arab-speaking people is the Bedouins. Bedouins are nomads. That means they do not stay in one place for a long time. They raise camels, horses, sheep, and goats. Some Bedouins stay at an oasis just long enough to collect the crops.

Another group of nomads living in the desert is the Tuaregs. At one time they were strong fighters. Today they raise herds of camels, goats, and sheep.

The Tuareg men wear a strip of blue cloth around their head that covers everything but their eyes. Their name means "People of the Veil."

The Gobi desert stretches across parts of Mongolia and China. Most of the desert is rock. Parts of the Gobi are very cold.

Mongol nomads live in tents called yurts. They often raise cattle, sheep, and goats. Many Chinese are farmers. They live in houses made from clay bricks.

Aborigine man

Once the Aborigines were the only people in the Australian deserts. They were nomads who lived in small groups. They moved from water hole to water hole. The Aborigine men hunted for the group's food. They tamed wild dogs called dingos to help them.

There are Bushmen living in the Kalahari desert in Africa. They live in much the same way as they did a hundred years ago. They travel across the desert looking for water and food. The Bushmen use bow and arrow to hunt. The arrows have poison on the tips to kill the animals.

Bushman

There are few
roads or paths in
the desert. This
makes it hard for
people to travel. At
one time, the only
ways to cross the
desert were on foot
or on camel.

Arabian camel

Although the camel is still used to carry heavy loads, its wool, hide, milk, and meat are also used by people.

Camels store fat in their humps. They can go without eating or drinking water for several days.

Bactrian camel

A camel with one hump is called an Arabian camel. It is the kind of camel that lives in Africa. The camel's long legs and wide feet help it walk on sand.

The Bactrian camel has two humps. Herds of Bactrian camels roam the deserts in central Asia.

Sometimes a sandstorm makes it hard to travel in the desert. Camels have two rows of eyelashes to protect their eyes from the sand. They also can close their nostrils so they don't breathe any sand.

sandstorm

mirage

People crossing the desert face many dangers. They can help protect themselves from the sun by wearing long, loose-fitting clothing. But there is also the danger of lack of water.

A mirage is when light makes an object look like something else. The light may make it look like there is a lake. But there really is no lake.

Today there are special machines that make it easier to cross the deserts. Jeeps and trucks are made for traveling in rough places. They have wheels that can move easily through the sand.

Modern machines also help workers dig wells to get to the oil under the desert.

Miles of pipeline carry oil across the desert. Ships then take the oil to places where it is made into many useful things.

There is not enough rain for crops to grow in the desert. Water has to be brought to the desert. This is called irrigation.

Sometimes water is found under the desert floor between layers of rock. Wells are drilled through the rock to bring the water to the surface.

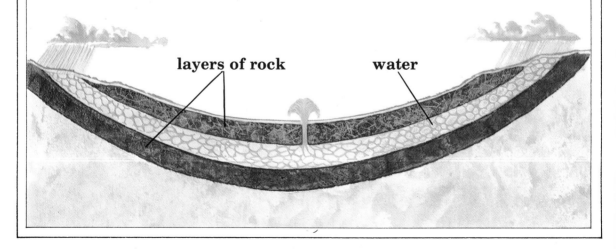

layers of rock   water

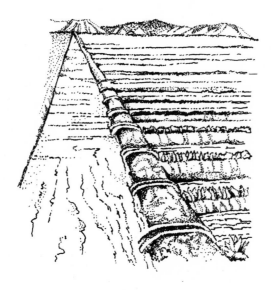

Other times water is taken from rivers and carried in pipes. Then it flows across the land in ditches.

Irrigation makes it possible for more people to use desert land for farming and raising animals.

The Metric System

In the United States, things are measured in inches, pounds, quarts, and so on. Most countries of the world use centimeters, kilograms, and liters for these things. The United States uses the American system to measure things. Most other countries use the metric system. By 1985, the United States will be using the metric system, too.

In some books, you will see two systems of measurement. For example, you might see a sentence like this: "That bicycle wheel is 27 inches (69 centimeters) across." When all countries have changed to the metric system, inches will not be used any more. But until then, you may sometimes have to change measurements from one system to the other. The chart on the next page will help you.

All you have to do is multiply the unit of measurement in Column 1 by the number in Column 2. That gives you the unit in Column 3.

Suppose you want to change 5 inches to centimeters. First, find inches in Column 1. Next, multiply 5 times 2.54. You get 12.7. So, 5 inches is 12.7 centimeters.

Column 1	Column 2	Column 3
THIS UNIT OF MEASUREMENT	TIMES THIS NUMBER	GIVES THIS UNIT OF MEASUREMENT
inches	2.54	centimeters
feet	30.	centimeters
feet	.3	meters
yards	.9	meters
miles	1.6	kilometers
ounces	28.	grams
pounds	.45	kilograms
fluid ounces	.03	liters
pints	.47	liters
quarts	.95	liters
gallons	3.8	liters
centimeters	.4	inches
meters	1.1	yards
kilometers	.6	miles
grams	.035	ounces
kilograms	2.2	pounds
liters	33.8	fluid ounces
liters	2.1	pints
liters	1.06	quarts
liters	.26	gallons

Where to Read About
Deserts

Aborigine (ab′ ə rij′ ə nē) *p. 23*

Arabian camel (ə rā′ bē ən   kam′ əl) *p. 27*

Australian desert (ôs trāl′ yən   dez′ ərt)
  p. 23

Bactrian camel (bak′ trē ən   kam′ əl) *p. 27*

barchan (bär′ kän′) *p. 7*

Bedouin (bed′ ə wən) *p. 20*

bobcat (bob′ kat′) *p. 15*

Bushman (boosh′ man) *p. 24*

camel (kam′ əl) *pp. 26-28*

date palm (dāt   päm) *p. 19*

desert owl (dez′ ərt   oul) *p. 14*

dingo (ding′ gō′) *p. 23*

dune (doon) *pp. 6-7*

elf owl (elf   oul) *p. 16*

Gobi (gō′ bē′) *p. 22*

irrigation (ir′ ə gā′ shən) *pp. 32-33*

jerboa (jər bō′ ə) *p. 16*

Joshua tree (josh′ ə wə   trē) *p. 12*

Kalahari (kal' ə här' ē) *p. 24*

kangaroo rat (kang' gə roo' rat') *p. 14*

kit fox (kit foks) *p. 15*

mirage (mi räzh') *p. 29*

oasis (ō ā' sis) *pp. 18-19*

ocotillo (ō' kə tē' yō) *p. 12*

oil (oil) *p. 31*

rattlesnake (rat' əl snāk') *p. 14*

saguaro (sə gwär' ō) *p. 13*

Sahara (sə har' ə) *pp. 20-21*

sandstorm (sand' stôrm') *p. 28*

scorpion (skôr' pē ən) *p. 17*

spadefoot toad (spād' foot tōd) *p. 17*

Tuareg (twä' reg') *p. 21*

yurt (yooərt) *p. 22*

Pronunciation Key

a	a as in **cat, bad**
ā	a as in **able**, ai as in **train**, ay as in **play**
ä	a as in **father, car**, o as in **cot**
e	e as in **bend, yet**
ē	e as in **me**, ee as in **feel**, ea as in **beat**, ie as in **piece**, y as in **heavy**
i	i as in **in, pig**, e as in **pocket**
ī	i as in **ice, time**, ie as in **tie**, y as in **my**
o	o as in **top**, a as in **watch**
ō	o as in **old**, oa as in **goat**, ow as in **slow**, oe as in **toe**
ô	o as in **cloth**, au as in **caught**, aw as in **paw**, a as in **all**
oo	oo as in **good**, u as in **put**
o͞o	oo as in **tool**, ue as in **blue**
oi	oi as in **oil**, oy as in **toy**
ou	ou as in **out**, ow as in **plow**
u	u as in **up, gun**, o as in **other**
ur	ur as in **fur**, er as in **person**, ir as in **bird**, or as in **work**
yo͞o	u as in **use**, ew as in **few**
ə	a as in **again**, e as in **broken**, i as in **pencil**, o as in **attention**, u as in **surprise**
ch	ch as in **such**
ng	ng as in **sing**
sh	sh as in **shell, wish**
th	th as in **three, bath**
t͟h	th as in **that, together**

GLOSSARY

These words are defined the way they are used in this book

although (ôl thō′) in spite of; even though

area (er′ ē ə) a certain place or part of
   something

below (bi lō′) to a place under or lower than

blown (blōn) to have been moved or carried
   by wind

breathe (brē<u>th</u>)   to take air into the lungs
   and then send it out

bury (ber′ ē) to put something in a hole
   and cover it

cactus (kak′ təs) a desert plant with a
   thick stem and branches that are covered
   with spines instead of leaves

centimeter (sen′ tə mē′ tər) a measure
   of length equal to .39 inches

central (sen′ trəl) placed in, at, or near
   the middle point or part of anything

claw (klô) a sharp, curved nail on an
   animal's foot

clay (klā) a fine earthy material that can be easily shaped when it is wet and hardens as it dries

climate (klī′ mit) the average weather, including temperature, wind speed, and rainfall, at a place over a period of time

clothing (klo′ <u>th</u>ing) things that are worn to cover the body

collect (kə lekt′) to bring several things together

common (kom′ ən) usual; happening many times

crop (krop) plants that are grown to be used for something helpful such as food

cross (krôs) to go from one side of something to another

desert (dez′ ərt) a dry, usually hot, place with little plant or animal life

ditch (dich) a long, narrow hole that is dug in the earth

drill (dril) to dig a hole in

dune (do͞on) a hill or mound of sand piled
   up by the wind
eyelash (ī′ lash′) one of the hairs that
   grows along the edge of the eyelid
fighter (fī′ tər) one who fights
flow (flō) to move along in a steady stream
foot (foot) the end part of the leg upon
   which a person stands
form (fôrm) to make or take shape
gather (ga<u>th</u>′ ər) to bring several
   things together
grown (grōn) to have been made to grow
growth (grōth) something that grows or
   has grown
herd (hurd) a group of animals
hide (hīd) the skin of an animal
huge (hyo͞oj) very large; great in size
hump (hump) a soft, fatty, rounded mound
   on the back of some animals
hundred (hun′ drid) the number 100
irrigation (ir′ ə gā′ shən) the act of
   supplying land with water

jeep (jēp) a small, powerful car that can move easily over rough land

lack (lak) something that is needed or wanted

layer (lā′ ər) one thickness or fold of something lying over or under another

loose-fitting (lōōs′ fit′ ing) something that is not tight in fit

lose (lōōz) to no longer have; to fail to keep

main (mān) the most in size or importance; chief

meter (mē′ tər) a measure of length equal to about 39 inches

mirage (mi räzh′) an image caused by the bending of light rays that looks like a pool of water, a mirror, or some other object

modern (mod′ ərn) like or belonging to the present time

moon (mōōn) the heavenly body that moves in a circle around the earth

nomad (nō′ mad) one of a group of people who moves from place to place to find food

nostril (nos′ trəl) one of the outer openings in the nose

oasis (ō ā′ sis) an area of desert land with a supply of fresh water that has a growth of plant and animal life around it

object (ob′ jikt) something that can be seen or touched; thing

oil (oil) a greasy substance that does not mix with water

parallel (par′ ə lel′) to go in the same direction at the same distance apart and never meet

period (pēr′ ē əd) a length of time

pipe (pīp) a long, hollow piece of material shaped like a tube

pipeline (pī′ plīn′) a line of pipe that is used to carry a liquid or gas

poison (poi′ zən) something that can cause sickness or death

poisonous (poi′ zə nəs) to be able to cause sickness or death by poison

quarter (kwôr′ tər) one of four equal parts that make up a larger whole

rainfall (rān′ fôl′) all the rain that falls on a place during a certain time

rainwater (rān′ wô′ tər) water that has fallen as rain

ridge (rij) a long, narrow raised strip

roam (rōm) to go from place to place without direction

root (ro͞ot) the part of a plant that grows underground

rough (ruf) having a bumpy, uneven surface

sandstorm (sand′ stôrm′) a kind of storm with strong winds that blow clouds of sand into the air

scaly (skā′ lē) to be covered with or made up of scales; fish are scaly

shade (shād) a place where there is little or no sunlight

skin (skin) the outer covering of a person's or some animal's body

soak (sōk) to take in a great deal of liquid and hold it

soil (soil) the top level of ground where plants grow

source (sôrs) the thing from which something begins or comes

stem (stem) the main part of a plant from which leaves, flowers, and fruits grow

stinger (sting′ ər) the sharp, pointed part of some insects or animals that is used to wound

strip (strip) a long, thin piece of a material

supply (sə plī′) to give something that is wanted or needed

surface (sur′ fis) the top or upper level

tame (tām) to change something from a wild state to a gentle state

themselves (<u>th</u>em selvz′) the same ones

thousand (thou′ zənd) the number 1,000

toad (tōd) a froglike animal that spends more time on land than in the water

travel (trav′ əl) to move from one place to another place

useful (yōōs′ fəl) helpful; having a good use

veil (vāl) a thin piece of cloth worn as a cover for the head and face

wax (waks) a substance produced by some plants and animals that is soft and easily shaped

wild (wīld) anything that grows naturally without the help of people

woodpecker (wood′ pek′ ər) a kind of bird that uses its long, hard bill to make holes in trees to find insects for food

wool (wool) the soft, curly hair of some animals that is spun into yarn and made into cloth

worker (wur′ kər) one who works

worn (wôrn) to have wasted away slowly

yellowish (yel′ ō ish) to be like the color yellow

Bibliography

Burton, Maurice. *Deserts*. Levittown, N.Y.:
Transatlantic Arts, Inc., 1975.

Goodheart, Barbara. *Year on the Desert*. Englewood
Cliffs, N.J.: Prentice-Hall, Inc., 1969.

Johnson, Sylvia A. *Animals of the Deserts*.
Minneapolis, Minn.: Lerner Publications Co.,
1976.

Kirk, Ruth. *Desert Life*. New York: Doubleday and
Co., 1970.

May, Julian. *Deserts: Hot and Cold*. Mankato,
Minn.: Creative Educational Society, Inc., 1971.

Pitt, Valerie, and Cook, David. *A Closer Look at
Deserts*. New York: Franklin Watts, 1975.

Pringle, Laurence. *The Gentle Desert: Exploring
an Ecosystem*. New York: Macmillan Publishing
Co., Inc., 1977.

Tyler, Margaret. *Deserts*. New York: John Day and
Co., 1970.